Contents

"From start to finish the scenery and countryside were glorious; shaded forests, sunny beaches, open moorland and fascinating railway tracks with high bridges and viaducts. Also; just the right amount of amenities en-route to keep the body and spirit fresh while preserving the peace and tranquility. Comfortable surroundings made the whole trip a family holiday (2 adults and 4 children of which the youngest only 7 years of age) to remember."

Gary and Jill Campbell, Addis Ababa, Ethiopia.

CU00564368

1

Introduction to the Devon Coast to Coast Cycle Route

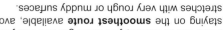

The Devon Coast to Coast cycle route is one of the best developed cycle routes of southern England. Most of the route is on well maintained cycle paths on dismantled railway lines, offering great views of the Devon countryside. It features four famous cycle paths; the Tarka Trail, Granite Way, Drake's Trail and Plym Valley Way, all with their own charms. These trails ensure the climbing is kept to a minimum, with only the occasional steep gradient to conquer. Hills do not dominate the route, making it achievable for all. Also; what goes up, gets to go down!

The total distance of the whole route is relatively small. Active cyclists will be able to ride the route in two to three days. If you are new to touring by bike, want to see all the sights, or when cycling with children, you should plan four to six days to cycle the route. This will give you plenty of time to do sight-seeing on the way, including some great walks. The Devon Coast to Coast Cycle Route is signposted as National Cycle Route 27, but with this guidebook we endeavour to give you more than just the official route, taking you to the best landmarks nearby. Also, if you follow our directions, you won't get lost and you'll be staying on the smoothest route available, avoiding stretches with very rough or muddy surfaces.

You can cycle the route in both directions. In this book, we describe the route from north to south. In the north, Barnstaple is the main gateway to get onto the route. The total distance is approximately 190 kms or 117 miles and we have split the route into three sections; Ilfracombe-Barnstaple, Barnstaple-Hatherleigh and Hatherleigh-Plymouth. Most people will do the ride between Barnstaple and Plymouth, a worthy "coast-to-coast" journey, with good connections for onward journeys on both ends. The first section, from Ilfracombe to Barnstaple, is less travelled, as it has some logistical challenges (see page 7).

It is worth making the effort to do (part of) the first section though. When also doing all the walks (see page 9), it is easy to spend three days here in itself. Ilfracombe has a very scenic harbour and is now a famous for its Verity Statue. Heading out of town, it is a very steep climb, so you could consider starting your ride in Woolacombe. Its fabulous beach could be a stunning start of your ride (see picture) and the ride up into the hills is more gradual, especially easier to accomplish with children. You'll have great vistas towards Exmoor on the way to Braunton, from where it is a flat ride on the Tarka Trail to Barnstaple.

Still, don't worry if you skip the first section. You'll also find stunning coastal scenery on the **second section** from **Barnstaple** to **Hatherleigh**. The Tarka Trail hits the North Devon Coast at **Instow**. "Little white town" **Bideford** is the gateway to the splendid beach of **Westward Ho!** and charming **Appledore**. Once you have rejoined the Tarka Trail, the old railway route follows the Torridge valley, criss-crossing the river several times. It doesn't take long before you'll get the feeling you are away from it all. Your journey through **Tarka County Park** can take you via **Torrington** and the popular **Puffing Billy** and **Yarde Orchard** cafes/budget accommodations. Hilly lanes via Petrockstowe and Sheepwash villages take you to **Hatherleigh**.

The **third section** from **Hatherleigh** to **Plymouth** starts with a challenge. The route's most demanding hills are found on the lanes around **Hatherleigh**. Once you have reached **Okehampton**, the cycling becomes truly spectacular. The **Granite Way** guides you onto the impressive **Meldon** and **Lake** viaducts, with great views of **Dartmoor National Park**. Get a taste of its wilderness through an activity run by the YHA in Okehampton or via a walk at **Meldon Reservoir**.

From **Lydford**, you'll pass **Lydford Castle**, **Lydford Gorge** and **Brent Tor**, all worth extra exploring on foot. Bustling **Tavistock** is a beautiful old town, filled with shopping opportunities. This is also the birth place of Sir Francis Drake, so the next railway path is the **Drake's Trail**, with its spooky **Grenofen Tunnel** and amazing **Gem Bridge**.

Beyond **Yelverton** you have once again fantastic views over Dartmoor, building up to the final section of the route. That is the **Plym Valley Way**, a cycling heaven hidden in a stunning wooded valley. It guides you all the way to Plymouth's seafront, keeping you well away from this city's suburbs and traffic, directly to the pleasant old part of Plymouth, **The Hoe**. The **Smeaton's Tower** lighthouse, the **Citadel Fort** and **Barbican Harbour** are all overlooking the English Channel; great landmarks to finish a great ride!

How to use this guidebook

The Devon Coast-to-Coast Route is generally easy to follow, with well-signposted "Route 27"-signs. There is the odd missing or confusing signpost though and many nearby great walks or landmarks are easily missed. Also, there are stretches with poor surface and/or the signposting stops where you need it most. This is where the value of this book truly kicks in. The guide provides lots of practical information, allowing you to plan your journey and its logistics, either at home beforehand or on the spot. It gives you the choice to navigate by following the signposts, using the directions (north-south only) or by using the maps. The **directions** are written in such a way that you do not need a bike computer. Maps always match the directions on the same page. Further information is scattered around it.

If you prefer to navigate with a navigation device or app, we are happy to provide **GPS-tracks** of the main cycle route in this book at no extra charge. Contact us via email, quoting "D-CTC-2017" and we'll send you the tracks in a compressed zip-file within three working days. Download the file to a laptop or tablet and "extract all files", then move all tracks to your device, referring to its own manual.

At the start of all route sections, an **elevation chart**, showing the grading of the terrain, is provided. Note these charts are generalised for clarity and don't show every incline and decline. Many **steep gradients** are marked on the maps with **arrows**. These arrows point down hill! For every sub-section, **pictorials** show the cycling distances for that section, with different types of cycling conditions: ☞ (cycle path, 50%), ⚡ (quiet road, 41%), 🚗 (road with possibly fast moving traffic or regular traffic flow, 8%) and 🚗🚗 (busy main road, 1%), see also page 8.

The scale and style of the **maps** vary per page. Every map has the essential clarity to find your way around. Waypoints on the maps match the directions, ensuring you are aware of the map scale. For reasons of clarity we decided only to use **kilometres** on the maps and in the directions of this book; divide by 1.6 to get miles! If you have a bike computer, set it on kilometres for easy use of the directions (reset to zero where indicated). On the maps you'll also find letters, matching **facility listings** from page 35. These allow you to quickly find accommodations and/or bike repair shops on or near the route. When a service provider is further away, a dotted line on the map will direct you there, sometimes with extra directions in the listings.

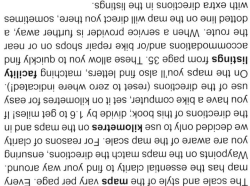

Key to used symbols and abbreviations

→	turn right
←	turn left
↑	straight on
↗	smooth turn right
↖	smooth turn left
↘	sharp turn right
↙	sharp turn left
↱	first turn right, then immediately left
↰	first turn left, then immediately right
🚲	cyclepath or cycle lane
	quiet road
🚗	road with possibly fast moving traffic or regular traffic flow
🚗🚗	busy main road; an adjacent footpath is always available!
	tourist attraction, view point or location of special interest
	beach or seafront promenade
	shop(s)
	cafe/pub with light refreshments
	pub/restaurant serving meals
	picnic area or bench(es) at prominent location
	hotel or bed & breakfast
	hostel, bunkhouse or yurts (YHA, YMCA or independent)
▲	campsite
	bike repair shop
(27)	National Cycle Route number (signposted)

Barnstaple	town, village, attraction or rural pub (note the name of a locality is in ***italic*** if there is a railway station)
T-jct	T-junction
jct	junction
cross rds	cross roads (four-ways junction)
rndabt	roundabout
ep	at end of path
1st rd	first road
2nd p	second path
lhts	traffic lights
car pk	car park
imm	immediately

street and road names abbreviations:

Br	Bridge	Ln	Lane
Cl	Close	Mt	Mount *or* Market
Cr	Crescent	Pd	Parade
Ct	Court	Pk	Park
Dr	Drive	Pl	Place
Gdns	Gardens	Rd	Road
Gn	Green	Sq	Square
Gr	Grove	St	Street
Is	Island	Tc	Terrace
		Wy	Way
		Wk	Walk

Brent Tor church near Lydford

Devon Coast to Coast logistics

Bringing your own bicycles by train via Exeter

If you bring your own bikes on the train, please note that trains have limited spaces for bikes. If you travel on long-distance trains to Exeter, make sure to make reservations for your bikes. There is normally no extra cost for this. Book via www.crosscountrytrains.co.uk or www.gwr.com. From London Waterloo to Exeter, bikes are taken on a "first come, first served" basis only, see www.southwesttrains.co.uk.

On the GWR-service Exeter-Barnstaple, there is also a "first come, first served" policy. Officially, there is space for two bikes only and during holiday periods this service is very in demand. Conductors normally try to get as many bikes on the train as possible, but it may well be that railway staff will make you wait for the next train. Trains between Exeter and Barnstaple run once per hour, on Sundays only once every two hours. We recommend only to carry bicycles on the Exeter-Barnstaple line before 3 pm or after 7 pm.

For long-distance trains on the Plymouth-Exeter-line, you'll need to make bike reservations. It is best to make bike reservations for your full journey home. Tickets are cheapest two to four weeks prior to travel. Travel times for the train journeys Exeter-Barnstaple and Plymouth-Exeter are both about one hour.

Bringing your own bicycles by car

Due to the one-way nature of the route, it is best to park your vehicle in Exeter, travelling to Barnstaple and back from Plymouth with bicycles on the train. Overnight parking on the Exeter "Park & Rides" is not permitted and long stay parking at Exeter St. Davids station is expensive. Free on-road parking is possible in housing estates west of Exeter St. Davids and near Digby & Sowton station, all at own risk. Park sensibly!

If you have more than two people with bikes, it may be worth to have you and the bikes taxied between Exeter and Barnstaple to avoid "train trouble". "Devon by bike" is a taxi service based in Exeter with a bike trailer, catering for parties up to six riders and bikes, see www.devonbybike.com, phone 01392 555247.

Hiring bicycles

For short distance hire, see the listings of rentals from page 35. Barnstaple's Tarka Trail Cycle Hire rents out bikes for the full route and will collect in Plymouth at the end of the ride, see www.tarkabikes.co.uk, phone 01271 324202. Okehampton's YHA offers two-day rentals (with transfer to Barnstaple on day 1 and collection in Plymouth on day 2, you sleeping 3 nights at their YHA), see www.yha.org.uk, phone 01837 53916.

Luggage transfers and full package holidays

If you want to cycle the route luggage-free, check out www.luggagetransfers.co.uk or call 01326 567247. Full package holidays (everything arranged, with up to six cycling days) can be booked via our own EOS Cycling Holidays; see www.eoscycling.com for details.

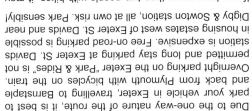

From Barnstaple to Ilfracombe (or Woolacombe)

Probably the biggest decision you have to make is whether to start in Barnstaple (easy) or whether to start in either Ilfracombe or Woolacombe. Have a good read on pages 10-15 to learn about the Ilfracombe - Woolacombe - Barnstaple route section before making up your mind. If you want to cycle this section, you'll have to get bicycles and people from Barnstaple to Ilfracombe (or Woolacombe). Tarka Trail Cycle Hire (www.tarkabikes.co.uk, phone 01271 324202) and Carb Cycles (www.carbcycles.co.uk, phone 01271 346316), both based in Barnstaple, are happy to transfer bikes and riders; advanced bookings are essential.

Of course you can also **cycle** between Barnstaple and Ilfracombe (or Woolacombe). Naturally, you can cycle the official route twice, but experienced cyclists may prefer a circular route. In that case, our suggested route to Ilfracombe is shown on this page. Most of this 20 km (12½ miles) route is on quiet lanes, but there will be some fast moving traffic when heading out of Barnstaple and coming into Ilfracombe. Also, the gradients on this route are long and steep. This route is **not** part of the Coast-to-Coast route and **unsuitable** for "easy riders" and most children.

From Plymouth Hoe to Plymouth station

Plymouth Hoe is the end of the sign-posted Devon Coast to Coast Route 27. This guidebook provides a quiet on-road route, linking Plymouth Hoe with Plymouth railway station.

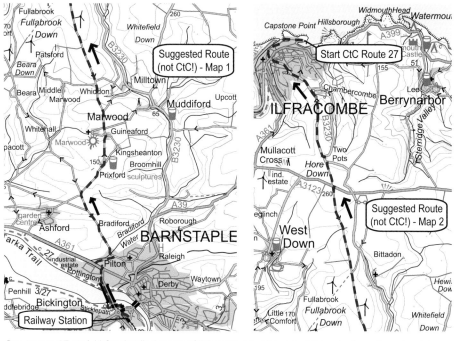

See pages 17 and 11 for detailed maps of this route heading out of Barnstaple and coming into Ilfracombe. The map used in this book is for sale at Tarka Trail Cycle Hire at Barnstaple station.

Travel information, equipment and your cycling style

Travel information

The Coast to Coast can be cycled all year round, but you'll get the best of the weather from Easter until mid-October. Attractions, cafes and accommodations can be shut during the winter period. Always be ready for cold wind and rain showers, whenever you travel.

Services on the way, such as shops, pubs, cafes, bike repair shops and attractions, are referred to in the route directions with symbols (for key see page 5). In rural places, the facility will be mentioned with its own name. In villages and towns however, you'll only find the name of the village or town with the appropriate symbols. This allows you to **see at a glance** how far it is to the next en-route facility. Always carry some food and drink so you are not caught out in rural areas.

The listings from page 35 feature accommodations and bike repair shops/rentals. Accommodations are only listed if these allow one-night stays. Venues with a minimum stay of two nights or more are omitted. Campsites and budget accommodations (such as youth hostels and bunk houses) are listed as much as possible where these are relevant for the route. B&Bs and hotels are only listed when these are directly on the route. Booking ahead for weekend dates and at sites in popular coastal areas is recommended.

Equipment

The Coast to Coast is best cycled on a hybrid bike with at least 18 gears to be able to deal with climbs. Bikes with narrow racing tyres will struggle on gravel sections, but alternative tarmac routes are suggested on the maps. A standard waterproof handlebars holder is recommended, as this book is designed to fit in such holders. If you carry your own luggage, pannier bags, with a rack on top of the back wheel, are recommended. If you intend to do camping with your own tent, you may also need a rack on the front wheel to carry more pannier bags. Special bikes, such as tandems, recumbent bikes, tricycles etc. will be fine to use (bear in mind the hilly sections), but there are some tricky to pass **barriers**. There are **steps** en-route in Ilfracombe and on the Bideford-Westward Ho!-route. Also, it may be difficult to bring special equipment on trains.

Your cycling style

On **quiet roads** (🚲 41 %) the biggest risk for a cyclist is being hit by cars moving in and out of driveways and sideroads. Always cycle in a position where you are visible for other road users. As a rule, you should keep at least one metre away from the road side. If you hear a car approaching from behind, try to move out to the middle of your side of the road before the vehicle gets close and make eye contact with the driver. This will force the driver to slow down and to overtake you wide as he/she should. On narrow lanes, hold cars behind you until you see a space to pull in which feels safe for you. Avoid cycling through narrow gaps; go wide around parked cars and large vehicles. Also, adjust your speed according to visibility, surface and weather conditions. Occasionally you'll find yourself on roads with a regular flow or fast moving traffic (🚗 8 %) or on a busy main road (🚗 1%). Either enforce your presence if you keep riding or just walk your bike!

Cycle paths (🚶 50 %) are always shared with pedestrians and they always have priority over cyclists. Always slow down and ring your bell or make some friendly noise when approaching from behind. Pass people wide and slow as much as possible. Take extra care around dogs, horses and children. If you have to travel via a public footpath, you must always dismount.

Walking the South West Coast Path and Dartmoor

There are some great reasonably short walks to make while cycling the Devon Coast to Coast. Walking can bring a pleasant break from cycling and sometimes you see more on foot. Most footpaths are narrow, with uneven surfaces, not suitable even to walk bikes along. Wear good shoes, always lock up bikes against a solid object and take valuables with you. Usually, it should be fine to leave pannier bags on the bikes, but try to put the lock through the bags' strings too. Dirty laundry on top in the bags will discourage theft! On this page, the finest walks on the way are listed north-south. Start points of the walks are listed in the cycling route directions; refer to the maps and general text to find your way. All times are return trips at easy pace.

Ilfracombe: ½ - 2½ hours (route 1, page 11):
Lock bikes up on the Pier for all walks. Go for an easy walk to **Capstone Hill**; westbound via the Victorian coast path, back via the town centre (½ hour). The harbour is best viewed from the cliffs above at **Larkstone**; walk around the harbour to the east to get there. The Larkstone tearooms are slightly inland on the way back (1 hour). You can extend this walk to the **Hillsborough** headland, site of an Iron Age Promontory Hillfort and now a Local Nature Reserve. This walk provides great views over Hele Bay further east. Return inland via the Larkstone tearooms (2 hours).

Morte Point: 2 hours (route 1, page 12):
Circular walk from **Mortehoe** on the South West Coast Path, with spectacular views over the Bristol Channel, Atlantic Ocean and Woolacombe beach. Lock bikes near Mortehoe village square or at the car park.

Woolacombe: up to 2 hours (route 1, page 12):
Walking the full length of **Woolacombe beach** to the Putsborough end and back will take about 2 hours.

Baggy Point: 3 hours (route 1, page 12):
Similar to Morte Point, but longer, with great views over both Woolacombe and Croyde beaches. Lock up bikes on the fence just south of **Putsborough beach**. On arrival in Croyde, you can also visit its beach. The route back is best via the public path on "Pathfields" road on your left. It takes you to Stentaway Lane.

Braunton Burrows: ½ - 3 hours (route 1, page 14):
England's largest unspoilt sway of sand dunes and amazing **Saunton Sands**, a UNESCO Biosphere Reserve, form a unique habitat and are worth the short detour from the Tarka Trail. See page 14 for full info.

Westward Ho!: 1 & 1 ½ hours (route 2, page 20/21):
Two walks take in the beauty of **Westward Ho!** and the **Northam Burrows Country Park**, both on the South West Coast Path. Walk one starts in the town centre, walk two at Sandymere, see pages 20/21.

Putsborough beach & White Lady fall (Lydford Gorge)

Meldon Reservoir: 1 hour (route 3, page 28):
The wilderness of **Dartmoor** is not easy to access by bike, but from the splendid **Meldon Viaduct** you can do a magnificent walk to Meldon Reservoir. You will also walk the reservoir's dam; a great picnic spot!

Lydford Gorge: 2x ½ or 2 hours (route 3, page 29):
Spectacular Lydford Gorge is the deepest valley in Southwest England. The walk features waterfalls and whirlpools of the River Lyd. The full circular route takes two hours, but you can make two half-hour walks, one from each entrance, taking you to the best features.

Brent Tor: ½ hour (route 3, page 29):
Brent Tor is a weathered volcano, topped by a 13th century church. It is a ten minute walk to the top of the hill. Visit the church and have a picnic on the hill's slopes. The views over Dartmoor are just amazing!

Route 1: Ilfracombe - Barnstaple: 40 Km / 25 miles

Route 1 takes you to the **North Devon Coast Areas of Outstanding Natural Beauty**. This spectacular coastal area, which covers some 66 square miles from the boundary of Exmoor National Park at Combe Martin to Marsland Mouth on the Cornish border, was designated as an AONB in 1960. The North Devon AONB is nationally protected for the beauty of its landscape and is overseen by a Partnership of local organisations who deliver a Management Plan. It is made up of several distinct landscapes, each with their own special habitats and geology with many of them receiving extra protection in their own right. **Ilfracombe** is such a special place. Make your way to the scenic harbour and its **Pier** to start the route. At the end of the Pier, you'll find the colossal statue of **Verity** by contemporary artist **Damien Hirst**. The statue has become a famous landmark since it was installed in 2012 and depicts a pregnant woman, holding the sword of truth and the scales of justice. Before you start cycling it is worth exploring the area around Ilfracombe Harbour on foot. Do at least one of our scenic Ilfracombe **walks**, see page 9.

From the pier, you can also join the **Ilfracombe Princess Cruise**, allowing you to view the coast from the sea and to spot seals and porpoises (weather dependent, call 01271 879727, from £10 pp). The cycle route takes you via the distinctive **Landmark Theatre** with its two domes to the entrance of the **Tunnels Beaches**. The tunnels helped to turn Ilfracombe from a fishing village into a seaside resort in the 1820s, taking you to its best, otherwise inaccessible, beaches (open daily, £3 pp). Heading out of town, you'll have to **carry bikes** on steps, but you can avoid them (see map). It is a steep rise onto the first section of **Tarka Trail**, which climbs alongside the green **Slade** valley. Up in the hills, go for the coastal route, unless you have narrow racing tyres. It takes you to **Mortehoe** with the stunning **Morte Point** and to majestic **Woolacombe**. Explore its beach and don't hesitate to hire a board and wetsuit from one of the **surfing** outlets. A gravel coastal path takes you to **Putsborough** (for the **Baggy Point walk**) and **Georgeham**, where you can see the house where the book **Tarka the Otter** was written (see page 24).

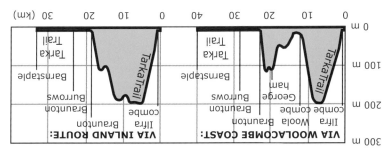

VIA WOOLACOMBE COAST: Ilfracombe – Woolacombe – Braunton – Barnstaple / Tarka Trail

VIA INLAND ROUTE: Ilfracombe – Braunton – Barnstaple / Tarka Trail

(0m / 100m / 200m / 300m; 0 10 20 30 40 / 0 10 20 30 (Km))

1a: Ilfracombe - Woolacombe Junction (7 km / 4½ miles)

🚲 5.0 km, 🚶 1.8 km, 🚗 0.5 km, 🚗🚗 0.0 km

Note, when arriving by train in **Barnstaple**, first turn to pages 16 and 17!

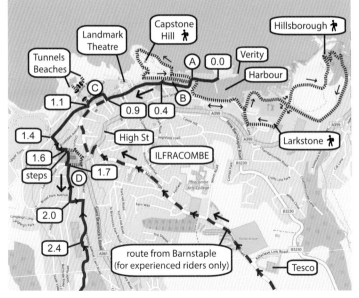

0.0 At 🚲🏠🚉📷🍴🚶 **Ilfracombe Pier**, at Devon CtC sign on toilets wall, go west, leaving pier (**27**)

0.4 At end of through rd (becomes one-way), ↑ (**27**) 🚗

0.9 After 🚲📷 ℹ️ **Landmark Theatre**, 1st rd → (Runnacleave Cr, *"no entry" road with* 🚲 *contra flow,* **27**)

1.1 Imm after entrance 🚲📷 ⚓ **Tunnels Beaches** 1st rd ↗ (Torrs Pk, **27**)

1.4 2nd rd ← (**27**)

1.6 On steep slope up ↗ via path with steps, *dismount* (**27**), follow path ↑ across cemetery

1.7 Ep ← and imm 2nd rd → (Belmont Rd, **27**)

2.0 1st rd ← (**27**) and 1st rd → (**27**)

2.4 At end of rd, join 🚲 🡔 (Tarka Trail, **27**)

4.7 🚲 🪝 **Slade Reservoir** (*on right, down steps at 2nd reservoir*)

7.3 At crossing of main rd, *choose your route on next page!*

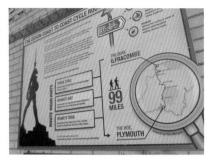

Look out for the Coast-to-Coast-sign on the Pier, on the wall of the public toilets. This is where the official route starts.

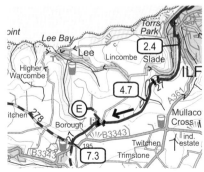

1b: Woolacombe Junction - Georgeham Junction

(via Woolacombe: 12 km / 7½ miles, inland: 6 km / 3½ miles)

via Woolacombe:	🚲 1.0 km,	🚗🚗 2.0 km,	🚶 9.0 km,	🚗🚗 0.0 km
inland route:	🚲 1.0 km,	🚗 0.8 km,	🚶 3.8 km,	🚗 0.0 km

7.3 Scenic coastal route via Woolacombe (1 km gravel or earth surface):

7.3 At crossing of main rd ← via 🚲 on right side of rd

10.4 In 🏕 ❧ ⚲ **Mortehoe**, keep ↘ via through rd
(For ⚲ Morte Point, walk starts 1st rd ← , then 1st footpath →)

12.4 At T-jct in front of the "Red Barn" pub, reset computer to 0.0:

0.0 Riders starting in 🏕 ❧ 🚲 🔔 🍴 ✉ 🅿 **Woolacombe:**
(12.4) In front of the "Red Barn" pub, go south ← via rd (Marine Dr, to Sandy Burrows, 278) (For 🏖 ⚲ beach ← after 100m)

0.3 After short climb → (Marine Dr, 278) (toll rd: free for 🚲!)

2.5 At end of Marine Dr, ↖ (Bridleway, to Putsborough)
poor surface in places, dismount where needed!

3.5 Ep ↑ via rd (278), 🔔 🚲 **Putsborough** on right side

3.7 (For ⚲ Baggy Point, walk starts uphill, 1st footpath →)

4.0 At jct, follow bend → (to Putsborough, 278), keep ↑

5.8 ❧ **Tarka The Otter House**
(Note; in 🏕 🚲 **Georgeham** look out for sharp bend to the right; Tarka The Otter house on left side of rd!)

5.9 At T-jct →, 1st rd ← (steep hill, to pub "The Rock", 278)

6.9 Stop at jct outside of village, merge routes, see next page!

Inland route, (all tarmac, staying high up):

7.3 Cross main rd ↑ onto 🚲
(to Braunton via roads, 27)

8.3 Ep ← via rd (27)
(to Braunton via roads, 27)

12.1 1st rd ↖ (to North Buckland, 27)

12.9 Stop at next junction, routes merge, see next page!

Scenery of the Morte Point Coast Path

Tarka The Otter House in Georgeham

HENRY WILLIAMSON WRITER (1895-1977) lived here from 1925 to 1929 and wrote "TARKA THE OTTER". Published 1927
THE HENRY WILLIAMSON SOCIETY

1c: Georgeham Junction - Braunton (5 km / 3 miles)

🚲 *1.2 km,* 🚶 *2.5 km,* 🚗 *1.4 km,* 🚗🚗 *0.0 km*

Heading south from Georgeham, you can't miss the majestic wind turbines of **Fullabrook Wind Farm**. The farm consists of 22 turbines. The turbines generate more than 100,000.00 MwH of electricity every year. Part of the farm's profits are put back into the community. On the map, between the current cycle route and Fullabrook, you can see a proposed **Tarka Trail extension** (in red colour). When built, it will be possible to cycle traffic-free from/to Ilfracombe, but this is not likely to happen until 2020 at the earliest (only Knowle-Braunton is open). Once you descend into **Braunton,** you can take in the vibe of surfing in the **Museum of British Surfing** (open daily, except Tuesdays, £4 pp) or browse one of Braunton's many surfing shops. **Salt Rock** is the popular local brand for surfing kit. Their outlet store can be found at Velator roundabout.

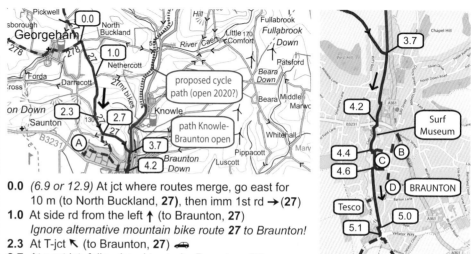

0.0 *(6.9 or 12.9)* At jct where routes merge, go east for 10 m (to North Buckland, **27**), then imm 1st rd → (**27**)

1.0 At side rd from the left ↑ (to Braunton, **27**)
Ignore alternative mountain bike route 27 to Braunton!

2.3 At T-jct ↖ (to Braunton, **27**) 🚗

2.7 At next jct, follow bend to ← (to Braunton, **27**) 🚗

3.7 At end of steep descent, *slow down*, → through gate onto 🚲 (to Village Centre, **27**)

4.2 Ep cross main rd 🛒 🛍 🍴 ℹ️ **Braunton** via lhts and → via 🚲, cross car pk access rd, then ↖ via 🚲 (to Barnstaple, **27**), 🏄 **Surf Museum** *(on left side of path after 50m)*

4.4 Keep ↖ at police station, cross tracks of railway crossing, at T-jct → (Station Rd, **27**)

4.6 1st rd → (Station Cl, **27**), imm ← via 🚲 (to Barnstaple, **27**)

5.0 Ep → cross rd via lhts and ← via 🚲 on right side of rd

5.1 At "Velator" rndabt, *choose route: Braunton Burrows, page 14, Barnstaple, page 15.*

1d: Braunton - Braunton /Burrows (7.8 km / 5 miles return)

🚴 *0.6 km,* 🚶 *7.2 km,* 🚗 *0.0 km,* 🚗🚗 *0.0 km*

Even if you intend to cycle from Barnstaple to Plymouth only, also try to cycle from Barnstaple to the **Braunton Burrows**. This is the core of the internationally designated UNESCO Biosphere Reserve and is one of many Sites of Special Scientific Interest in the North Devon Coast Areas of Outstanding Natural Beauty. It is England's largest sand dune system, known for its many habitats, supporting a range of species. The rare sand lizard and 33 different species of butterfly can be spotted here, as can a unique range of 400 plant species and birds. To maintain the diversity of life, scrub and grass is grazed by cattle and wet dune slacks are actively protected from overgrowing. The area can only be explored on foot. Walk at least to **Flagpole dune**, a distinctive sand dune, popular for sand tobogganing and with great views. Walk on to **Saunton Sands**, from where you can return to your bikes (one hour return). For a circular walk via the beach either south (anti-clockwise) or north (clockwise), allow three hours. In that case, follow South West Coast Path route signs from the beach back to the start point.

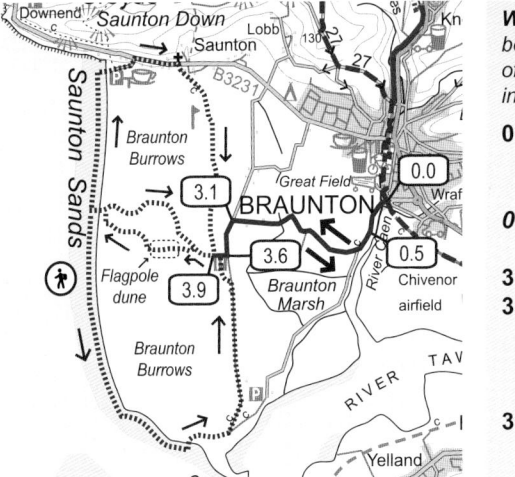

Warning: *Bring food and drink and be prepared for the exposed terrain of the Braunton Burrows. Also, obey instructions of military warning signs!*

0.0 *(5.1)* At "Velator" rndabt, go west via rd (see 🍴 **Salt Rock shop** on corner)

0.5 🍴⛵ **Velator Quay** *(on left side of rd),* keep ↑ via rd

3.1 At T-jct ← (no signs!)

3.6 At end of rd →, ↑ across Sandy Lane Car Pk, pass gate and continue on wide gravel path (Bridleway)

3.9 Gate 🚶 **Braunton Burrows** (lock bikes along fence), *after visit, same way back!*

1e: Braunton - Barnstaple (7.9 km / 5 miles one way)

🚲 7.9 km, 🚶 0.0 km, 🚗 0.0 km, 🚗🚗 0.0 km

The **Tarka Trail** between Braunton and Barnstaple is the busiest cycle path of North Devon, well-used by local commuters and visitors alike all year round. The path on the bed of the former Ilfracombe-Barnstaple railway opened in 1991. Near Braunton, the path is next to **Chivenor Airfield**. The military here is due to be replaced by new housing estates. Further east, the path provides continuous views over the **River Taw**, which is a tidal estuary all the way up to Barnstaple. At low tide, you'll find birds looking for food on the mud flats. Barnstaple's stylish high river bridge (with cycle path!) dates from 2007.

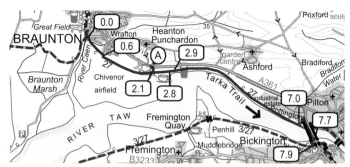

0.0 *(5.1 or 7.8)* At "Velator" rndabt, go south via 🚲 (to Barnstaple, Tarka Trail, **27**)

0.6 Ep ⬆, continue via 🚲 (see gate airfield, Tarka Trail, **27**)

2.1 At "Chivenor" rndabt ⬆ via 🚲 (to Barnstaple, **27**)

2.8 🍴🏪 **Riverside Cafe** *(on right side of path, see sign)*

2.9 🍴🏪 🍽 **Braunton Inn** *(pub on left side of path, see sign)*

7.0 At 🚲 jct, just before high river bridge, *choose route:*
For scenic circular route via Barnstaple town centre and station, see page 17.
For direct route to Bideford, see below:

7.0 ⬅ via 🚲 (to Bideford, **27**), ep ➡ onto high river bridge; use 🚲 on right side of main rd (to Bideford, **27**)

7.7 After high river bridge, 1st 🚲 ➡ (to Bideford, **27**)

7.9 At next 🚲 jct, end of route: *continue on page 18.*

Route 2: Barnstaple - Hatherleigh: 74 km / 45 miles

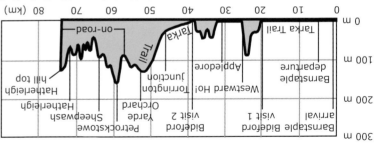

Route 2 starts in **Barnstaple**, the largest town in North Devon. The **Tarka Trail Cycle Hire** is conveniently located at the railway station. If you are just arriving for your Devon coast-to-coast journey, more information can be found here. The **station** used to be a major hub with various railways heading north, west and east. The railway to Exeter is the only surviving route today. Most old railways have been converted into cycle paths, making Barnstaple one of England's most cycle-friendly towns. Away from this cycle network, the traffic situations can still be challenging though, so keep to the cycle paths for enjoyable cycling!

Barnstaple plays a vital trading role in the region, which is reflected in the long **High Street** and the historic **Pannier Market** building. On most days of the week you'll find a thriving market here. A circular route, using the bridges of the River Taw, makes a pleasant stroll or bike ride, before heading on to Bideford. On "The Square" you'll find the **Barnstaple & North Devon Museum** (free entry). Locals love to spend time at **Rock Park**, also on the riverside cycle route.

2a: Barnstaple Circular Route (5 km / 3 miles)

🚲 4.9 km, 🚶 0.1 km, 🚗 0.0 km, 🚗🚗 0.0 km

Arrivals from Braunton start at top; arrivals at station, start at middle!

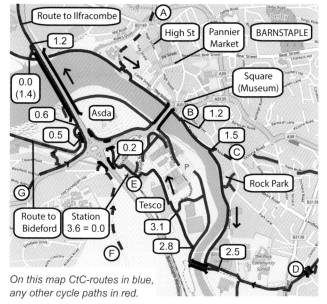

On this map CtC-routes in blue,
any other cycle paths in red.

0.0 *(1.4 or 7.0)* At 🚲 jct, just before high river bridge, go east via 🚲 (to Town Centre, **27 Link**), keep to riverside 🚲 route
1.2 At 🚶 🏠 🚏 📷 🍴 ℹ️ **Barnstaple** "The Square" ↗ via 🚲 (to Rock Park, **27**)
1.5 Keep ↗ via riverside 🚲 (**27**), 🚶 📷 **Rock Park** on your left
2.5 After 🚲 has left the riverside, 1st 🚲 ↘, make U-turn up bank to river bridge (to Station/Bideford, **3**)
2.8 After river bridge, 1st 🚲 ← (to Station, **3**)
3.1 Ep ↑ via rd (to Station, **3**), after 50m, join 🚲 ↑ on left side of rd
3.5 Ep cross rd ↗ onto 🚲 on right side of bus lane (to Station, **3**)
3.6 Opposite lhts of bus lane (main entrance station), *reset to* **0.0**:
0.0 *Riders starting from* 📷 **Barnstaple Railway Station:**
(3.6) Opposite station, on 🚲 (see lhts of bus lane), go west via 🚲, on right side of bus lane (to Tarka Trail, **3/27**)
0.2 Just before high viaduct over bus lane → via 🚲 (to Braunton, **3/27**), after subway ← via 🚲 (to Braunton, **3/27**)
0.5 At 🚲 jct after next subway, *choose your route:*
For direct route to Bideford, see page 18.
For scenic circular route via town centre and route to Ilfracombe, read below:
0.5 At 🚲 jct after subway ↑ (to Braunton, **3/27**)
0.6 Ep ← onto high river bridge; use 🚲 (to Braunton, **27**)
1.2 After high river bridge, 1st 🚲 ↙ (to Braunton, **27**)
(For route to Ilfracombe for experienced cyclists only: after high bridge ↑ via 🚲, at lths ↑ via 🚲, at next jct with lhts cross ↑ via 🚲, then ← via 🚲 on right side of rd, 1st → (Chaddiford Ln), at T-jct ←, see page 7)
1.4 At riverside 🚲 jct *reset computer to* **0.0**, *continue on top of this page!*

2b: Barnstaple - Bideford (15 km / 9 miles)

🚲 *13.2 km,* 🚶 *0.3 km,* 🚌 *1.0 km,* 🚗🚗 *0.0 km*

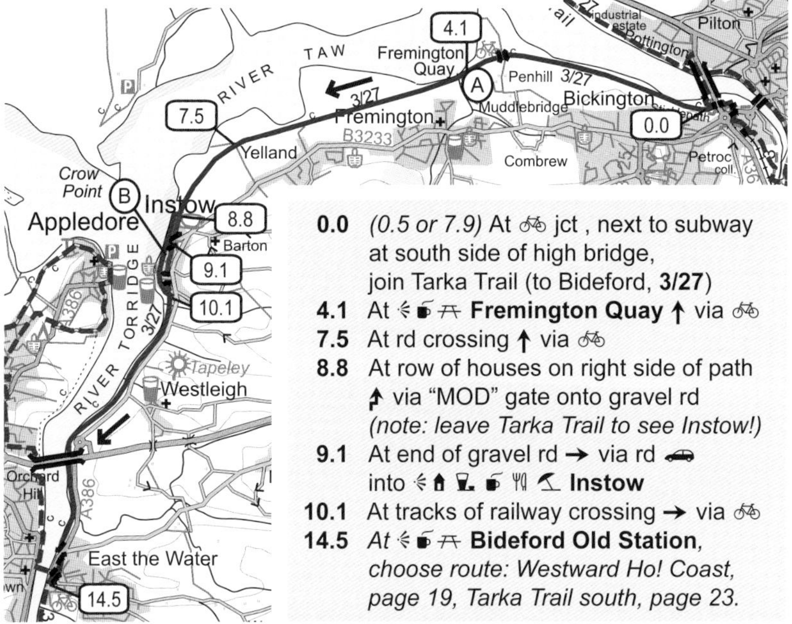

The **Tarka Trail** between Barnstaple and Bideford is not the busiest cycle path on the Coast-to-Coast when looking at figures of all-year round usage, but it gets very crowded on sunny days in the summer holidays and in weekends. On such days, you may find this section congested, with walkers, families, touring and racing cyclists all claiming their space. This truly flat section overlooks the Rivers Taw and Torridge most of the way. The best views of the Taw estuary are at **Fremington Quay**, a popular spot for a picnic or to hang out at the cafe. We recommend coming off the trail at charming **Instow**. This allows you to enjoy its beach and the views towards the Atlantic Ocean and Appledore. If you stay on the Tarka Trail (see the red line on the map), you won't see any of this. Leaving Instow, the Tarka Trail leads to Bideford, hugging the River Torridge all the way.

0.0 *(0.5 or 7.9)* At 🚲 jct , next to subway at south side of high bridge, join Tarka Trail (to Bideford, **3/27**)

4.1 At ⬕ 🚻 **Fremington Quay** ↑ via 🚲

7.5 At rd crossing ↑ via 🚲

8.8 At row of houses on right side of path ↑ via "MOD" gate onto gravel rd *(note: leave Tarka Trail to see Instow!)*

9.1 At end of gravel rd → via rd 🚌 into ⬕ 🏠 🛏 🍴 ⚓ **Instow**

10.1 At tracks of railway crossing → via 🚲

14.5 At ⬕ 🚻 **Bideford Old Station**, *choose route: Westward Ho! Coast, page 19, Tarka Trail south, page 23.*

2c: Bideford - Westward Ho! - Appledore - Bideford (18 km / 11 miles)

🚲 *2.5 km,* 🚶 *13.6 km,* 🚗 *1.2 km,* 🚗🚗 *0.6 km*

0.0 *(14.5)* Walk ↘ via steps with ramp, resume cycling ↑ via rndabt onto bridge 🚗🚗 *(See map for level alternative route for steps with ramp!)*

0.3 After river bridge → at rndabt and **dismount**; use lhts to cross rd ↟ onto quay 🚲, **resume cycling**, keep ↗ via 🚲 on quay ⛵ 🚉 🚏 🍴 ⚓ ℹ **Bideford**

0.7 At end quay 🚲, 1st rd ↗ (Riverbank Car Pk) *(For ⛵ ℹ **Burton Art Gallery** ↑)*

1.2 At end car park rd **dismount**; walk ↑ via path (South West Coast Path)

1.3 **Resume cycling** at "Riverbank House" on rd, at sharp bend to left ↑ via path (Coast Path), ↗ onto rd

1.6 At rndabt ↑ (Riverside Cl), at T-jct → (Chircoombe Ln), at end of tarmac ↖ via gravel rd (under high bridge)

1.8 At end of gravel rd ↑ via tarmac rd

2.0 At T-jct ← up steep hill (Limers Ln)

2.4 At T-jct → via 🚲 on right side of rd

"Little white town" **Bideford** has many shops in the streets behind its quay. In **Victoria Park** you can find the **Burton Art Gallery** (free). If you do not plan to see the coastal sights on route 1 (see pages 12 and 14), do not miss out on our route via **Westward Ho! beach** and **Appledore**.

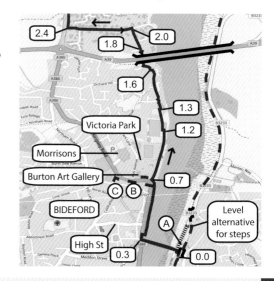

Westward Ho! is a town with an exclamation mark in its name. It was founded as a holiday park and named after a book published in 1855. The beach is one of Devon's best but during high tide it all disappears under the Atlantic waves. To catch a wave, rent a wetsuit and board from the local **surf school**. It is a steep climb to join the **Kipling Tors walk**, but your efforts are rewarded with fantastic views over the bay, especially when going all the way to the shelter on the cliffs. Walk back via the **South West Coast Path**, about a one hour round trip. Extend the coast path walk as you wish.

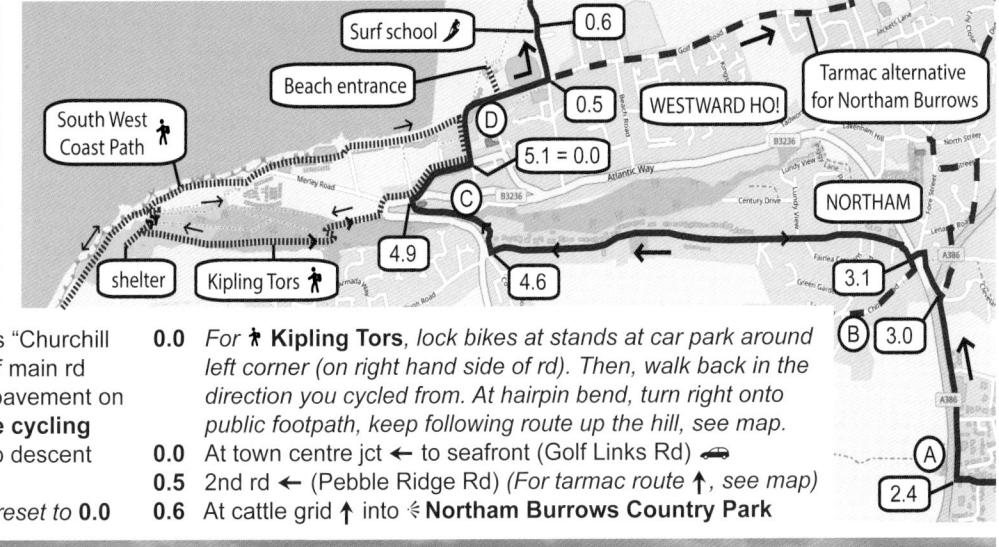

Surf school

Beach entrance

0.6

0.5

WESTWARD HO!

Tarmac alternative for Northam Burrows

South West Coast Path

D

5.1 = 0.0

C

NORTHAM

4.9

4.6

3.1

shelter

Kipling Tors

3.0

B

A

2.4

3.0 Ep ← (Cleveland Pk), **dismount** at T-jct, cross "Churchill Way" and walk ↑ via pavement on right side of main rd

3.1 At bus stop, cross main rd ↑, walk further via pavement on left side of rd, 1st rd ↖ (Bay View Rd), **resume cycling**

4.6 Just before "Stop"-sign → (Fosketh Hill), steep descent

4.9 At end of descent, at T-jct ↗

5.1 At town centre ⚐ 🏠 🏪 🛒 🍴 ⚓ **Westward Ho!** *reset to* **0.0**

0.0 *For* 🚶 **Kipling Tors**, *lock bikes at stands at car park around left corner (on right hand side of rd). Then, walk back in the direction you cycled from. At hairpin bend, turn right onto public footpath, keep following route up the hill, see map.*

0.0 At town centre jct ← to seafront (Golf Links Rd) 🚗

0.5 2nd rd ← (Pebble Ridge Rd) *(For tarmac route ↑, see map)*

0.6 At cattle grid ↑ into ⚐ **Northam Burrows Country Park**

Northam Burrows Country Park is a coastal area with salt marsh, grasslands and sand dunes. It is a dynamic place, next to the mouth of the Rivers Taw and Torridge. Being part of North Devon Coast Areas of Outstanding Natural Beauty, it is protected from development. Lock bikes at the stands opposite **Sandymere beach access** for a ninety-minute circular walk. Walk north via the beach or the coast path (depending on the tide). Make your way around the shallow inlet **Skern** and turn right just before the tarmac road's bridge onto the grassy path next to the stream. This will take you back to Sandymere.

1.6 At ⬕ 🚶 **Sandymere Beach Access** → via tarmac rd, keep going ↑

2.9 After exit with cattle grid, 1st rd ← (Appledore Rd, to Appledore), keep ↑

5.0 On arrival in **Appledore**, 1st rd ← (Jubilee Rd, to "Toilets"), at next jct ↖ to view point ⬕ 🚻 **Skern** *(mouth Rivers Taw & Torridge)*

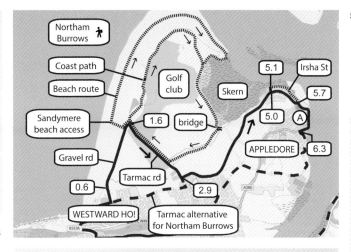

5.1 From view point ⬕ 🚻 **Skern** back to through rd via Jubilee Rd and turn ← onto through rd **OR** **dismount** and walk via Hillcliff Tc against one-way flow, with estuary on left side into ⬕ **Irsha Street**

Irsha Street is a street with very scenic cottages, directly built on the side of the estuary. The narrow street has a one-way flow in the opposite direction, so you shouldn't cycle here. Walking bikes in the opposite flow is allowed though! This walk will only take about five minutes. At its end, you will rejoin the through road, which you can also use if you want to keep cycling. **Appledore** has a lively quay, popular for crabbing. For high-quality fish and chips, visit **Sylvesters**, see sign on the quay.

5.7 In ⬕ 🏠 🛍 🍴 ⬕ **Appledore** ↑ via Esplanade 🚗

6.3 At end of Esplanade, at 1st rd ↙ (Newquay St) *reset to* **0.0**, *continue on next page*

Via Appledore's ship yards and Northam village, our route takes you back to Bideford and the Tarka Trail. Away from the occasional pub or café you won't see any shops directly on the route until you arrive in Hatherleigh; buy essentials in Bideford!

0.0 *(6.3)* At end of Appledore Esplanade, 1st rd ↗ (Newquay St), keep ↑, next to ship yards (gradual climb)

1.5 At T-jct ↕ cross main rd (Primrose Ln)

1.8 In steep descent, follow bend to ↖, then imm 1st rd → (Diddywell Rd), keep ↑ into residential area of Northam

2.8 In 🍴 **Northam** ↓ via square 🍴, 1st rd → (Cross St)

3.0 1st rd ← (Burrough Rd)

3.2 At T-jct ←, 1st rd → (Castle St, dead end rd), **dismount** at end, join footpath

3.4 Cross main rd ↕ to footpath on left side of rd, follow path in between two walls and **resume cycling**, at next jct ↑ via 🚲 on left side of main rd

4.0 3rd rd, just before sign of large rndabt, → (Limers Ln)

4.5 In steep descent via tarmac rd ← (Chircoombe Ln), where tarmac rd bends to right ↑ via gravel path *(steep descent, poor surface, please dismount)*, eg ↗

4.7 1st rd →, and at rndabt ↑ via residential area

5.1 Where road bends to the right ↓ via path ("Coast Path"), at "Riverbank House" on your left, **dismount**, ↑ via path

5.3 At skate park, rejoin rd and **resume cycling**, keep ↖

5.7 At T-jct ↑ via 🚲 on quay ↕ 🍴 🚲 ♨ 🛏 🍴 **Bideford**

6.2 At end of quay 🚲 via rot → onto bridge 🚲 🚲

6.5 After bridge at rndabt →, imm **dismount** on corner, via steps with ramp to ↕ 🚲 ♿ **Bideford Old Station,**
(See map for level alternative route for steps with ramp!)

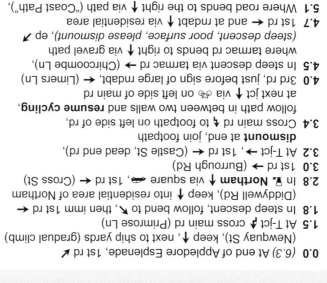

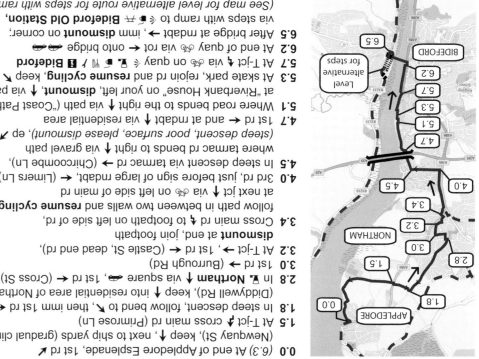

Level alternative for steps

2d: Bideford - Great Torrington (8 km / 5 miles)

🚲 *8.4 km,* 🥾 *0.0 km,* 🚗 *0.0 km,* 🚗🚗 *0.0 km*

South from Bideford, the **Tarka Trail** is at it's best. Depending on the tides, you could navigate the River Torridge yourself by kayak at **Bideford Kayak Hire** (open daily, from £15 pp). Also when cycling the trail, you'll find the narrowing Torridge valley stunning. You'll cross the river several times and there is also a tunnel, taking you very close to **Great Torrington** at **Puffing Billy Station** with its cafe and bike rental. Great Torrington town lies at the top of a long and steep hill. Those who make the effort to do the climb will find the tiny **Pannier Market** charming. In Great Torrington, you can also learn about glass making at **Dartington Crystal** (open Mon-Fri, £8 pp).

0.0 *(6.5 or 14.5)* From **Bideford Old Station**, go south via Tarka Trail 🚲 (to Torrington, **3/27**)

8.3 At 🚲 🍴 ⚲ **Puffing Billy & Torrington Cycle Hire** ↑ via 🚲 (**3/27**), go on path under viaduct

8.4 At 🚲 **Taddiport Junction** (just after viaduct) *choose route: Tarka Trail south, see next page. For* 🚶 🏠 🛏 🚲 🍴 ℹ️ **Great Torrington** *(2 km):* → *through gate (to Taddiport), imm* ← *via gravel path, keep* ↑ *through factory area, ep* ↟ *start steep climb "Mill St", keep* ↑ *to town centre*

2e: Great Torrington - Hatherleigh (28 km / 17 miles)

🚲 12.7 km, 🥾 15.2 km, 🚐 0.0 km, 🚐🚐 0.0 km

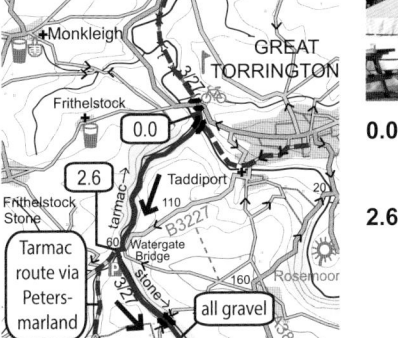

+Monkleigh

GREAT TORRINGTON

Frithelstock

0.0

2.6

Frithelstock Stone

Taddiport
110

Watergate Bridge
60

B3227

tarmac

Rosemoor

160

Tarmac route via Petersmarland

all gravel

Smytham

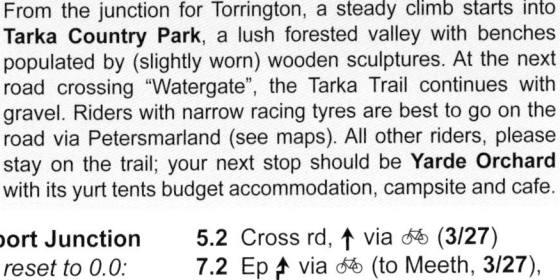

From the junction for Torrington, a steady climb starts into **Tarka Country Park**, a lush forested valley with benches populated by (slightly worn) wooden sculptures. At the next road crossing "Watergate", the Tarka Trail continues with gravel. Riders with narrow racing tyres are best to go on the road via Petersmarland (see maps). All other riders, please stay on the trail; your next stop should be **Yarde Orchard** with its yurt tents budget accommodation, campsite and cafe.

0.0 *(8.4)* At 🚲 **Taddiport Junction** (just after viaduct) *reset to 0.0:* ↑ via 🚲 (to Hatherleigh, **3/27**)

2.6 Ep → and imm ← onto car park, ↑ via 🚲 (**3/27**) *(For tarmac route at ep →, follow signs via Petersmarland, then to Sheepwash, see maps)*

5.2 Cross rd, ↑ via 🚲 (**3/27**)

7.2 Ep ↑ via 🚲 (to Meeth, **3/27**), 🏠 ⛺ ☕ 🍴 **Yarde Orchard**

12.5 At 3rd rd crossing beyond Yarde Orchard (Moormill) ↑ onto rd (to Petrockstowe, **3/27**) *(note: ignore Tarka Trail to Meeth, see info next page)*

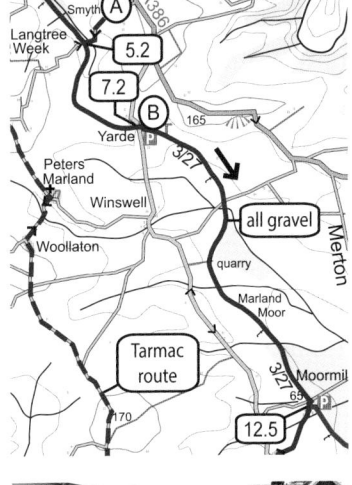

Smyth A386

Langtree Week
5.2

7.2

B

Yarde 165

Peters Marland

Winswell

Woollaton

quarry

Marland Moor

Tarmac route

Moormill

12.5

all gravel

Merton

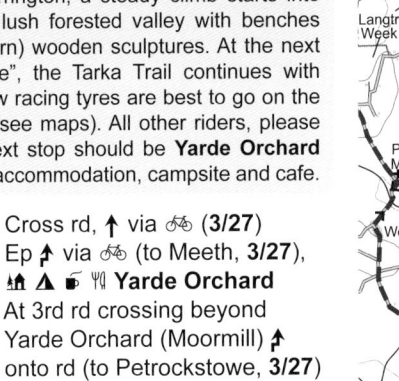

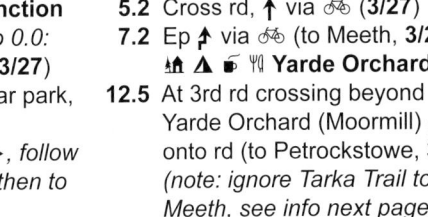

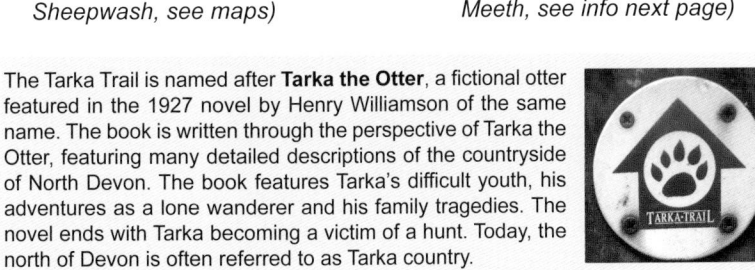

The Tarka Trail is named after **Tarka the Otter**, a fictional otter featured in the 1927 novel by Henry Williamson of the same name. The book is written through the perspective of Tarka the Otter, featuring many detailed descriptions of the countryside of North Devon. The book features Tarka's difficult youth, his adventures as a lone wanderer and his family tragedies. The novel ends with Tarka becoming a victim of a hunt. Today, the north of Devon is often referred to as Tarka country.

TARKA-TRAIL

Beyond **Moormill**, there is a bit more of Tarka Trail to go, but the route currently ends in Meeth, on the hazardous main road A386. Extension of the Tarka Trail to Hatherleigh is on its way, but the missing section is not likely to open until 2020 at the earliest. You should leave the Tarka Trail at Moormill, so you can ride the quiet roads via **Sheepwash**. From here, the route to **Hatherleigh** is truly hilly, probably the hardest section of the Coast-to-Coast. The signposted route was redirected to Highampton in recent years, but this new route is just as hilly as the old one and also exposes you to some fast moving traffic. We stick to the "old route" with our directions, the signposted "new route" is shown with a dotted line on the map.

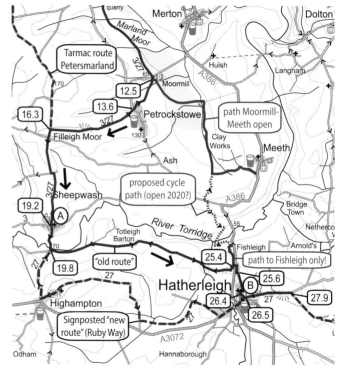

13.6 At jct ↑ (to Sheepwash, **3/27**) *(For* 🛏 🍴 *Petrockstowe pub* ←, *200m, uphill!)*

16.3 At T-jct ← (to Sheepwash, **3/27**), follow through rd
   (Note: tarmac road route via Petersmarland rejoins here)

19.2 In 🏠 🍺 🛏 🍴 **Sheepwash** *(pub and small shop)* ↑ (to Highampton, **27**)

19.8 Imm after river bridge, 1st rd ← (to Totleigh)
   (Note: ignore signs **27**, *unless insisting on cycling offical route, see above)*

25.4 At T-jct ← via path, then imm → cross main rd,
   → via gravel 🚲 up slope (to Hatherleigh), ep ← on tarmac

25.6 At T-jct → via rd

26.4 In 🏠 🍺 🛏 🍴 **Hatherleigh** *(various shops, pubs and cafes)*,
   in steep descent, at 🏠 🛏 🍴 **The George Hotel**, ← (High St), steep climb

26.5 At jct ↖ (Victoria Rd, **27**), steep climb *(Note: ignore Sticklepath 🚲 route)*

27.9 On top of hill, at 1st rd →, at ⚡ 🪑, end of route: *continue on next page*.

Route 3: Hatherleigh - Plymouth: 76 km / 47 miles

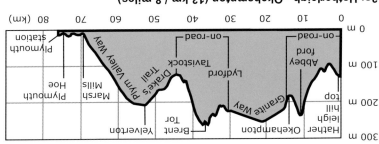

3a: Hatherleigh - Okehampton (13 km / 8 miles)

🚲 0.1 km, 🚶 12.7 km, 🚲 0.1 km, 🚲 0.1 km

The top of the hill east of Hatherleigh provides panoramic views towards **Dartmoor**. It is a rural country lane ride via **Abbeyford Woods** to Okehampton, with a long steady climb up.

0.0 (27.9) On top of hill, at 1st rd ←

3.2 1st rd ← (to Cadnam, 27) (to Upcott, 27)

4.9 At T-jct → 1st rd ← (to Woodhall, 27), (to Okehampton, 27), then imm 1st rd → (27)

8.5 At cross rds ↓ (to Hook, 27)

9.1 **Abbeyford Woods** (via car park on left)

10.9 At T-jct ← (to Okehampton, 27), keep going ↓ into town

Okehampton is a compact town, sitting in a valley right next to **Dartmoor National Park**. The **Okehampton Castle ruins** are slightly away from the town and our route, but worth a visit (open daily, £4 pp, English Heritage members free). Do all your shopping in town before heading up the steep hill to the old railway station, start point of the Granite Way cycle path. The **YHA** is located next to this station and runs many activities onto **Dartmoor**. Climbing, abseiling, caving, canoeing, raft building, archery, orienteering, weaselling (see picture) and a high ropes course are all available as half-day sessions; ideal to make a great day in combination with the cycling (www.yha.org.uk/okehampton-activity-centre, 01837 53916). Together with the Meldon Reservoir Walk (see next page), this is the best opportunity to get a good feel for southern England's last wilderness. Dartmoor is a desolate place, with only the occasional road or path going across it. The Granite Way (see next page) skirts the area on its side slopes. If you wish to explore the high grounds, get a good map. Orienteering skills are essential to avoid Dartmoor's notorious **bogs** and to find your way to the famous **Tors**.

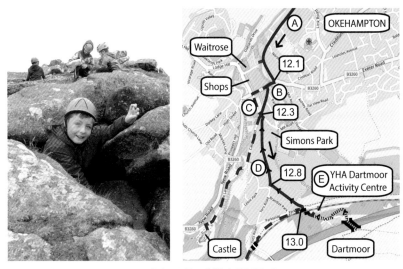

Lake Viaduct on the Granite Way

12.1 At T-jct → 🚗🚙 into ⛄🏠🏨🚻🛒🍴⚡🛈 **Okehampton**, after river bridge imm ←, onto pavement, beyond church ↑ via rd (**27**)

12.3 At square ↖ (Station Rd, **27**) *(For* ⛄**Okehampton Castle** *at square* ↑*)*

12.8 1st rd ↖ (Station Rd, **27**)

13.0 At Okehampton station entrance, in front of viaduct, *choose route:*
For ⛄🏨🚶 **YHA Dartmoor Activity Centre** ↑, *after tunnel imm* ↖
For route to Lydford via the Granite Way, see next page.

3b: Okehampton - Lydford (14 km / 8½ miles)

🚲 *13.7 km,* 🚶 *0.1 km,* 🚗 *0.0 km,* 🚗🚗 *0.0 km*

Start the **Meldon Reservoir Walk** via the steps down next to the railway carriage cafe. Then, cross the road, keep descending into the valley. When approaching the dam, go up on the left and cross the valley by walking the dam. From the dam, walk the road back to the Granite Way, up the ramp. Turn right on the cycle path to Meldon Viaduct.

The **Granite Way** was built on a railway line which closed in 1968. Now and then, heritage steam trains still run from Okehampton's old station to Meldon quarry. There is also a diesel service between Exeter and Okehampton during the summer on Sundays; otherwise rely on your bicycle! Except for a rough 200m gravel section (which can't be avoided) the Granite Way is all tarmac. Two deep valleys are crossed via the **Meldon** and **Lake Viaducts**, both masterpieces of Victorian engineering and providing superb views over Dartmoor. Do not miss out on the one hour **Meldon Reservoir walk** (see blue box on left).

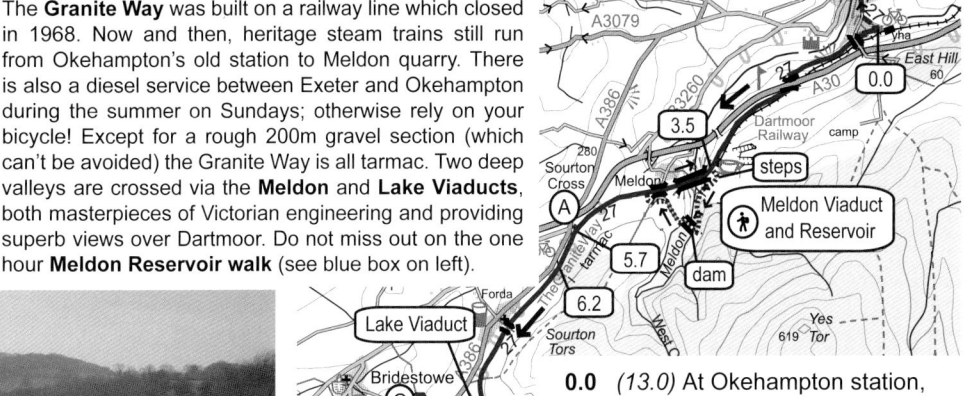

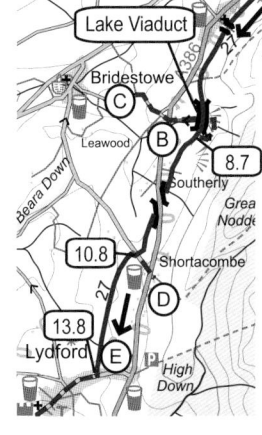

0.0 *(13.0)* At Okehampton station, go west via rd (to Lydford **27**), 1st 🚲 ↙ (Granite Way, **27**)

3.5 🚶🚲 **Meldon Viaduct/Reservoir** *For 🚶, lock bikes at stands at 🚲*

5.7 At ⛺ ⚲ **Sourton** ↑ via 🚲 (**27**)

6.2 Cross rd, ↑ via 🚲 (**27**)

8.7 🏠 🚲 🍴 **Bearslake Inn** *(pub, 800m from main route, ←)*

10.8 Cross rd, ↑ via 🚲 (**27**)

13.8 At 🏠 🚲 **Lydford Country House**, at ep, *continue on next page.*

3c: Lydford - Tavistock (16 km / 9½ miles)

🚲 0.5 km, 🥾 9.5 km, 🚗 5.5 km, 🚗🚗 0.0 km

Lydford is a friendly village featuring a medieval prison, the ruins of **Lydford Castle** (free access). You can also go for a spectacular walk in **Lydford Gorge**. This is the deepest valley in Southwest England. The entrance fee (£7 pp, National Trust members free) is steep, but worth it. Just as spectacular is the free walk onto exposed **Brent Tor.** For more info on both walks, see also page 9. Stick to our directions for the smoothest ride, but be ready for some fast-moving traffic. The signposted routes via Mary Tavy and the "summer route" are for mountain bikers only!

0.0 *(13.8)* From end of Granite Way → via rd **(27)**
0.8 At ⑂ 🚲 🍴 **Lydford** *(castle ruins & pub)* ↑ via rd
1.2 At ⑂ 🚶 🚲 **Lydford Gorge - Main entrance** ↑
2.9 Follow rd to → over narrow bridge **(27)**
  (Ignore signs "Summer Route 27" to the left!)
3.0 At ⑂ 🚶 🚲 **Lydford Gorge - White Lady entrance** ↑ via rd up the steep hill 🚗
5.2 Keep ↑ 🚗 *(Ignore signs route 27 to North Brentor, signposted route is via a rough section!)*
7.3 At ⑂ **Brent Tor** ↑ 🚗 *(For 🚶, lock bikes at car pk on right side of road, opposite footpath to church)*
8.5 In descent, 2nd rd ↖ **(327)**, keep ↑
12.9 Just before viaduct over the rd → via rd **(27)**

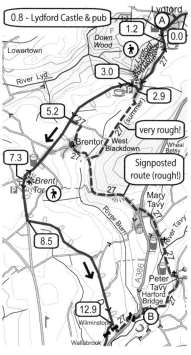

Dotted routes for mountain bikes only!

A long descent will take you into lively **Tavistock**. Choose between the main route through town (270) or the town bypass route (27). The bypass route leads over a high viaduct before it disappears in a deep cut. In this book, we describe the main route through town. Tavistock is popular for shopping, with the historic **Pannier Market** at its centre. There are also various **mews**; shopping streets only to be accessed via narrow gates from the main shopping street. **Bedford Square** is the central square, with many monumental buildings, such as the town hall and the Bedford Hotel. Both were built in the days that mining of copper brought prosperity to the town. Tavistock's most famous son is **Sir Francis Drake**, second in command when defeating the Spanish Armada in 1588. The next cycle path on the Devon Coast to Coast Route, the **Drake's Trail**, is named after him and will take you to **Yelverton**.

13.6 After viaduct over the rd, 1st ⟵⟶ ↗ (27)

14.1 After ⟵⟶ ⚲ **Wallabrook Viaduct** at ep → via rd

14.8 In descent, just before viaduct over the road, choose your route: To bypass Tavistock town centre, ↙ via ⟵⟶ (270), follow signs route 270, see map! For main route, via Tavistock town centre, keep ↓, go under viaduct, in descent 1st rd ⤴ (Barley Market St)

15.3 At T-jct → into High St ⟵⟶ ↑ 🍴 🚲 🅿 🏧 ↗ **Tavistock**, then 1st rd ⟵ (Market Rd)

15.5 Dismount at T-jct, continue on next page

Town views from Tavistock Viaduct

Meadowlands Park

Route 27

Bedford Sq

15.5

Pannier Market

15.3

A · B · C

Route 270 (bypass)

Tavistock Viaduct

14.8

14.1

Wallabrook Viaduct

13.6

TAVISTOCK

The **Drake's Trail** is built in challenging terrain on the course of an old railway. To reopen its **Grenofen Tunnel**, a bat colony had to be relocated. Another problem was the missing link of **Walkham viaduct**, which was blown up in 1965 by the army. To be able to cross the deep valley, a new bridge had to be built from scratch. Stunning **Gem Bridge**, part-funded by the EU, has become the symbol of hard work and long-term commitment to build the Devon CtC-route.

3d: Tavistock - Yelverton (9 km / 5 miles)

🚲 *7.9 km,* 🚶 *1.0 km,* 🚗 *0.0 km,* 🚗🚗 *0.0 km*

0.0 *(15.5)* At end of Market Rd (arrival Bedford Square) **dismount**, cross rd via lhts, walk ←, after bridge → **resume cycling** on 🚲 in park (St Johns Av, **27**)
0.3 At car pk ↗ via narrow path (to Meadowlands Pool)
0.5 Ep → via narrow bridge, then imm ← (**27**)
0.6 After playground ⛲ **Meadowlands Park** ↗ via wide path (**27**), leading to tunnel, ↑ via 🚲 (**27**)
1.7 Cross rd, ↑ via 🚲 (**27**)
1.9 Ep ↟ (West Devon Business Park, **27**)
2.0 At end of rd via 🚲 ramp ↗ to rndabt, cross 🚦 rd ↖, onto 🚲 on right side of main rd (**27**)
2.1 Cross main rd ↟ via lhts, continue via 🚲 (**27**)
2.3 Ep ↟ (Hazel Rd, **27**), at end of rd ↑ via 🚲 (**27**)
2.5 Ep →, 1st rd ↖, at end 🚲 ← via rd (**27**)
2.9 At T-jct ← (**27**), imm ↗ via 🚲 (to Plymouth, **27**)
6.5 Ep ↑ via residential rd
6.9 Ew ↑ onto 🚲 (**27**)
8.6 Cross rd ↑ via 🚲 (**27**), (🚦 ☕ 🍴 *pub & shop on left*), cross car park ↟, continue via 🚲 (**27**)
8.9 At rndabt 🏨 🚦 ☕ 🍴 **Yelverton**, *continue on next page*

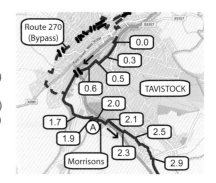

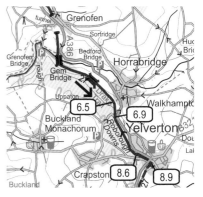

3e: Yelverton - Plymouth Marsh Mills (14 km / 8 miles)

🚲 11.8 km, 🚶 1.8 km, 🚗 0.0 km, 🚗🚗 0.0 km

Yelverton with its enormous roundabout feels like a service station and for cyclists to Plymouth it is. There are no shops directly on the route until Plymouth's city centre. It is great to have a picnic on the heights just west of **Clearbrook**, with your last panoramic views over Dartmoor. After passing the pub in this village, you join the superb **Plym Valley Way**. This cycle path takes you through another long tunnel and four more high viaducts; cycling paradise it is! To honour all the former railways you have been cycling, you could join the **Plym Valley Railway** for a short steam train ride, near the south end of the trail (£4 pp, every hour, most Sundays only).

0.0 *(8.9)* At rndbt, cross A386 rd to Plymouth, → via 🚲, imm ↑ onto lay-by rd (**27**), becomes 🚲 (**27**)
1.0 Ep ← via bridge, imm → (Clearbrook, **27**), ↑ onto 🚲
3.4 Ep ← onto rd, down hill (**27**)
4.0 In 🛏 🍴 **Clearbrook** *(pub)*, 1st rd → (to Plymouth, **27**),
4.1 1st 🚲 → (to Plymouth, Plym Valley Way, **27**)
11.7 Ep, cross car pk ⛶ **Plym Valley Railway**, ↗ via 🚲 (**27**)
13.6 Ep, *continue on next page*

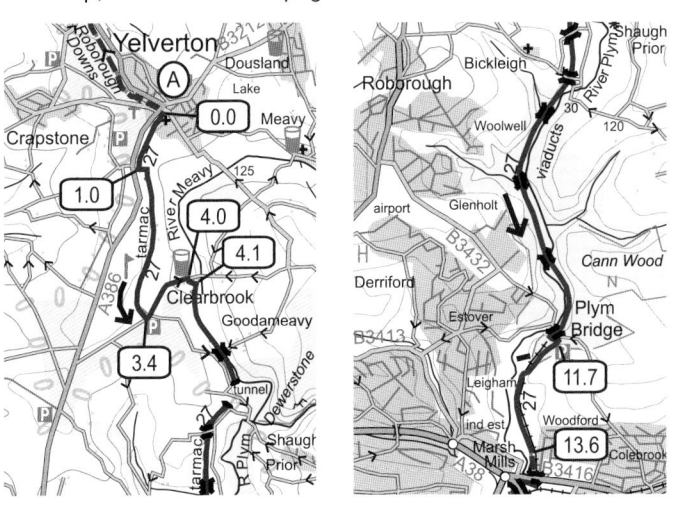

3f: Plymouth: Marsh Mills - The Hoe - Station (11 km / 7 miles)

🚲 *5.3 km,* 🚶 *4.1 km,* 🚗 *1.6 km,* 🚗🚗 *0.3 km*

The route arrives in Plymouth at **Marsh Mills**. Choose here between a full tarmac route on the west side of the Laira Estuary (recommended for those on narrow tyres) or the scenic, gravel official route on the east side of the water. The official route allows you to visit **Saltram House**. Mostly created between 1740 and 1820, the house and gardens in rural setting are well worth exploring (gardens and cafe open daily, £6pp, house open Sat&Sun, £11pp, National Trust members free). Routes merge at the Laira Bridge, from where you travel via the working **Cattedown Docks** and a short section of the **South West Coast Path** to the **National Marine Aquarium** (open daily, £12 pp). After you have walked the locks of historic **Barbican Harbour**, look left to descend the **Mayflower Steps**. This is where you can dip your feet in the water at the same spot from where the famous Mayflower ship set sail for the New World!

On this map CtC-routes in blue, any other cycle paths in red.

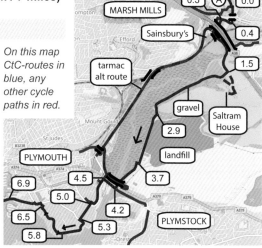

MARSH MILLS · Sainsbury's · tarmac alt route · gravel · Saltram House · Mount Gould · St Judes · PLYMOUTH · landfill · PLYMSTOCK · Orestor
0.5 · A · 0.0 · 0.4 · 1.5 · 2.9 · 3.7 · 4.5 · 5.0 · 4.2 · 5.3 · 6.9 · 6.5 · 5.8

0.0 *(13.6)* Ep ↑ via rd, at T-jct ↰ via 🚲 (**27**) *(do not cross railway!)*

0.4 Ep → via 🚲 on left side of rd (to City Centre, **27**)

0.5 1st 🚲 ← (to Plympton, **27**), keep ↑ (to Hoe, **27**) *(For tarmac route and 🛒 store ↑ via 🚲, next 🚲 ←, see map)*

1.5 In park, 1st gravel path → (**27**) *(For 🚶🛒 **Saltram House** ↑)*

2.9 Ep ↗ via tarmac rd (**27**)

3.7 At T-jct ↗ via 🚲 (to Hoe, **27**)

4.2 Ignore signs of route **27**, keep ↑, at lhts → via 🚲 on left side of rd onto wide bridge (to Hoe, **27**)

4.5 At lhts ← via 🚲 on right side of rd (to Cattedown Wharf, **27**)

5.0 At rndabt ← (Maxwell Rd, **27**)

5.3 At T-jct ← (Cattedown Rd, **27**), follow sharp bend to →

5.8 At end of rd ↑ via 🚲 (South West Coast Path, **27**)

6.5 Ep ↖, at T-jct ← 🚗, in bend ↖ (to Lock Gates, **27**), keep ↑

cross main rd via bridge to 🚲 🚶 **Plymouth Station**

1.6   **Dismount** at end of rd, walk ↗ to bus stop,
1.4   1st rd ← (Bayswater Rd)
       at rd **resume cycling** → 🚲
1.2   **Dismount** at house no 3 on Archer Pl, walk ↑ (park on right),
0.7   At mini rndabt ↑, at top of hill via bend →, keep ↑
0.5   At rndabt cross main rd ↑ (Octagon St, to "R.C. Cathedral")
0.3   At rndabt ← (to Exeter) 🚲
0.0   (9.5) At rndabt ↙ (to Continental Ferry Port) 🚲🚲
9.5   At rndabt reset to **0.0**; End of Devon Coast-to-Coast, for station:
8.5   At rdabt ↑, keep following coastal rd, keep going ↑ (27)
8.0   At rndabt ↖ (to "Boat Trips", 27)   (For ⅃ **Hoe** & ⅃ **Citadel** ←)
7.4   At T-jct ↖ (Madeira Rd, to Hoe, 27) 🚲
       (For ⅃ 🚲 ⚑ 🍴 ⛽ 🏨 **Barbican** →)
7.2   After locks and ⅃ **Mayflower Steps** → (27), **resume cycling**
6.9   At end 🚲 **dismount** to walk ↑ through lock area,

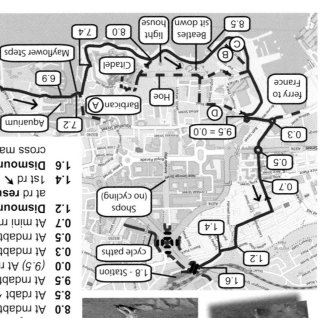

Map labels: Aquarium · Barbican A · Hoe · Citadel · Mayflower Steps · light house · sit down house · Beatles · ferry to France · B · C · D · Shops (no cycling) · cycle paths · Station · 9.5 = 0.0 · 7.2 · 6.9 · 7.4 · 8.0 · 8.5 · 0.3 · 0.5 · 0.7 · 1.4 · 1.2 · 1.6 · 1.8

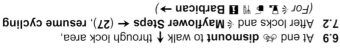

Barbican is the place to dine and drink. Opposite the Mayflower Steps, the **Mayflower Museum** provides historical context (open daily, £3 pp). At the Tourist Information in the same building you can also book for guided tours in the **Citadel**, the old military stronghold overlooking the harbour (£5 pp). Once you have reached the **Hoe**, you can stick to the pleasant Esplanade or cycle up to the wide green. Hang around and sit down on the grass as the **Beatles** once did (see seats at the Hoe's west end) or visit the monumental **Smeaton's Tower** lighthouse (open Tue-Sat, £3 pp). Stick to the Hoe area, unless you fancy shopping in the huge arcade that forms the city centre. Cycling is not permitted here. Use our route to cycle to Plymouth Station once Route 27 ends.

Facility Listings

The listings below should by no means be regarded as a full overview of Bed & Breakfasts, guesthouses, hotels, hostels, campsites, bike repair shops and bike rentals on the route. The facilities haven't been visited by us in person, but they appear to be generally suitable (see also page 8).

Pricing indication for ♠ B&Bs/Hotels and ♠♠ Hostels/Bunkhouses/Yurts:
£   £60 or less per night for a shared room with 2 people
££   between £60 and £80 per night for a shared room for 2 people
£££ more than £80 per night for a shared room for 2 people
Note: Solo travellers pay up to 80% of prices above for a single room!

Pricing indication for ▲ Campsites:
£   £10 or less per night for one person
££   more than £10 per night per pitch for one person (price often per pitch)

↘ Accommodation located in reasonably quiet and peaceful surroundings
≈ Accommodation located near noisy traffic or street/venue noise (people)

Rte	Km	Page	Ref	Town	Info	Name, address and postcode	Phone	Internet	Distance to route & extra directions
1a	0.1	11	A	Ilfracombe	♠ ≈ £££	Harbour Lights B&B, 26 Broad St, The Quay, EX34 9BL	01271 862778	www.harbourlightsbandb.co.uk	-
1a	0.1	11	A	Ilfracombe	♠ ≈ £££	Royal Brittannia Hotel, Broad St, EX34 9EE	01271 862939	www.royalbritannia.co.uk	-
1a	0.4	11	B	Ilfracombe	♠♠ ≈ £	Ocean Backpackers Hostel, 29 St James Pl, EX34 9BJ	01271 867835	www.oceanbackpackers.co.uk	0.1 km (at end of one way-rd ↘)
1a	1.0	11	C	Ilfracombe	♠ ↘ £££	Carlton Hotel, Runnacleave Rd, EX34 8AR	01271 862446	www.ilfracombecarlton.co.uk	-
1a	1.8	11	D	Ilfracombe	♠ ↘ £	The Darnley Hotel, 3 Belmont Rd, EX34 8DR	01271 863955	www.darnleyhotel.co.uk	-
1a	6.1	11	E	Ilfracombe	▲ ↘ £	Lea Meadow Farm, Shaftsborough Ln, Lee, EX34 8FF	01271 879825	www.leemeadowcamping.co.uk	0.4 km (← via car pk, ← via rd, 1st rd ←)
1b	9.3	12	A	Mortehoe	▲ ↘ £	Damage Barton, EX34 7EJ	01271 870502	www.damagebarton.co.uk	-
1b	10.4	12	B	Mortehoe	▲ ↘ £	North Morte Farm, EX34 7EG	01271 870381	http://northmortefarm.co.uk	0.6 km (in Mortehoe, 1st rd →)
1b	12.4	12	C	Woolacombe	♠ ≈ £££	The Rocks Hotel, Beach Rd, EX34 7BT	01271 870361	www.therockshotel.co.uk	0.2 km (at T-jct at Red Barn ↖ up the hill)
1b	6.2	12	D	Georgeham	♠ ↘ ££	Cozy Nights B&B, 16 Longland Ln, EX33 1JR	01271 890203	www.cozyknights.co.uk	0.1 km (after "The Rocks" pub, 1st rd →)
1b	10.2	12	E	Woolacombe Down	▲ ↘ ££	Little Roadway Farm, Georgeham Rd, EX34 7HL	01271 870313	http://littleroadway.co.uk	-
1c	2.7	13	A	Braunton	▲ ↘ ££	Lobb Fields, Saunton Rd, EX33 1HG	01271 812090	www.lobbfields.com	1.4 km (at jct ↑, 2nd rd → (Pixie Ln), T-jct ←)

Rte	Km	Page	Ref	Town	Info	Name, address and postcode	Phone	Internet	Distance to route & extra directions
1c	4.4	13	B	Braunton	♠ ≂ £££	The George Inn, Exeter Rd, EX32 2JJ	01271 814903	www.ohhpubs.co.uk/the-george-inn/	0.4 km (at T-jct ←, at T-jct ←, at T-jct ↘)
1c	4.4	13	B	Braunton	⚲	South Fork, 2 Exeter Rd, EX32 2JL	01271 817247	www.southforkracing.co.uk	0.5 km (at T-jct ←, at T-jct ←, at T-jct ↘)
1c	4.5	13	C	Braunton	hire	Otter Cycle Hire, The Old Pottery, Station Rd, EX33 2AQ	01271 813339	-	
1c	4.6	13	D	Braunton	♠ ⚲ ££	The Brookfield B&B, South St, EX33 2AN	01271 812382	www.thebrookfield.co.uk	0.2 km (follow bend ←, at T-jct →)
1c	4.6	13	D	Braunton	♠ ⚲ ££	Stockwell Lodge B&B, 66 South St, EX33 2AS	01271 817128	www.stockwell-lodge.co.uk	0.2 km (follow bend ←, at T-jct ↑)
1e	2.1	15	A	Chivenor	▲ ≂ £	Chivenor Caravan Park, 85 Chivenor Cross, EX31 4BN	01271 812217	-	0.1 km (at rndabt ←, at next rndabt ↑)
2a	0.7	17	A	Barnstaple	⚲	Carb Cycles, Pilton Causeway, EX32 7AA	01271 346316	www.carbcycles.co.uk	0.5 km (← via rd, see bend ↗, at rndabts ↑)
2a	0.7	17	A	Barnstaple	♠ ≂ £££	Yeo Dale Hotel, Pilton Bridge, EX31 1PG	01271 342954	www.yeodalehotel.co.uk	0.6 km (← via rd, see bend ↗, at rndabts ↑)
2a	1.2	17	B	Barnstaple	⚲+ hire	Bike It, The Square, EX32 8LS	01271 323873	www.bikeitbarnstaple.co.uk	-
2a	1.2	17	B	Barnstaple	⚲	The Bike Shed, The Square, EX32 8LS	01271 328628	www.bikeshed.uk.com	-
2a	1.5	17	C	Barnstaple	♠ ⚲ ££	Park Hotel, Taw Vale, EX32 9AE	01271 372166	www.brend-hotels.co.uk/thepark	0.1 km (at start Rock Park ↖ via rd)
2a	2.5	17	D	Barnstaple	♠ ⚲ ££	Poplars B&B, Rumsam Rd, EX32 9EW	01271 378773	www.barnstaplebedandbreakfast.co.uk	0.6 km (↑ ⚲ (3), at lhts ↑ ⚲ (3), 1st ↘, →)
2a	0.0	17	E	Barnstaple	hire	Tarka Trail Cycle Hire, Railway Station, EX31 2AU	01271 324202	www.tarkabikes.co.uk	-
2a	0.2	17	F	Barnstaple	♠ ⚲ £	Herton Farm B&B, Lake Hill, EX31 3HU	01271 323302	www.herton-guesthouse.co.uk	0.6 km (↑ via ⚲ under viaduct, ep ← via rd)
2a	0.6	17	G	Barnstaple	♠ ≂ ££	Cresta Guest House, 26 Sticklepath Hill, EX31 2BU	01271 374022	www.crestaguesthouse.co.uk	0.6 km (→ ⚲ along main rd, ↗ up hill via ⚲)
2b	4.0	18	A	Fremington	hire	Bike Trail Cycle Hire, Fremington Quay, EX31 2NH	01271 372586	www.biketrail.co.uk	-
2b	9.4	18	B	Instow	♠ ⚲ £££	Wayfarer Inn, Lane End, EX39 4LB	01271 860342	www.thewayfarerinn.co.uk	0.1 km (← opposite beach entrance)
2c	0.0	19	A	Bideford	♠ ≂ £££	Royal Hotel, Barnstaple St, EX39 4AE	01237 472005	www.brend-hotels.co.uk/theroyal	- (at station, opposite steps down, at rndabt)
2c	0.7	19	B	Bideford	⚲	Cycles Scuderia, Kingsley Rd, EX39 2PF	01237 476509	www.cyclesscuderia.co.uk	0.1 km (cross main rd ←, Pill Rd)
2c	0.7	19	C	Bideford	♠ ⚲ ££	Corner House B&B, The Strand, EX39 2ND	01237 473722	www.cornerhouseguesthouse.co.uk	0.2 km (cross main rd ←, Pill Rd, T-jct ←)
2c	2.5	20	A	Northam	♠ ⚲ ££	Old Barn B&B, Heywood Rd, EX39 3QB	01237 478704	http://oldbarnbideford.co.uk	-
2c	3.1	20	B	Northam	♠ ⚲ ££	Sundene House B&B, Chope Rd, EX39 3QE	01237 422950	www.sundenehouse.com	0.2 km (after crossing main rd ↑ to Chope Rd)
2c	4.8	20	C	Westward Ho!	♠ ⚲ ££	Culloden House, Fosketh Hill, EX39 1UL	01237 479421	www.culloden-house.co.uk	-
2c	0.3	20	D	Westward Ho!	♠ ≂ ££	Waterfront Inn, Golf Links Rd, EX39 1LH	01237 474737	www.waterfrontinn.co.uk	-
2c	6.0	21	A	Appledore	♠ ≂ £££	Seagate Hotel, The Quay, EX39 1QS	01237 472589	http://theseagate.co.uk	0.1 km (from the Quay →)
2c	6.1	21	B	Appledore	♠ ⚲ ££	Torridge House, 19 Bude St, EX39 1PS	01237 477127	www.torridgehouseappledore.com	-
2d	0.3	23	A	Bideford	hire	Bideford Cycle, Surf & Kayak Hire, Torrington St, EX39 4DR	01237 424123	www.bidefordbicyclehire.co.uk	- (leave Tarka Trail via ramp)
2d	8.3	23	B	Great Torrington	♠♠ ♠ ≂ £	Puffing Billy Trading Company, Station Hill, EX38 8JD	01805 623050	www.puffingbilly.co.uk	-
2d	8.3	23	B	Great Torrington	hire	Torrington Cycle Hire, Unit 1, Station Yard, EX38 8JD	01805 622633	www.torringtoncyclehire.co.uk	-
2d	8.4	23	C	Great Torrington	♠ ≂ £	Eastmond House B&B, 4 Potacre St, EX38 8BH	01805 623411	www.eastmondhouse.co.uk	2.0 km (see Torrington route, major climb!)
2d	8.4	23	C	Great Torrington	♠ ⚲ ££	Windsor House B&B, New Rd, EX38 8EJ	01805 623529	www.windsorhousebandb.co.uk	2.0 km (see Torrington route, major climb!)
2e	5.2	24	A	Little Torrington	▲ ⚲ £	Smytham Manor, EX38 8PU	01805 622110	www.smytham.co.uk	0.5 km (← at rd crossing, in climb 1st ←)
2e	7.2	24	B	Petersmarland	♠♠ ▲ ⚲ £	Yarde Orchard, East Yarde, EX38 8QA	01805 601778	www.yarde-orchard.co.uk	-